Simon & Schuster Canada
A Division of Simon & Schuster, Inc.
166 King Street East, Suite 300
Toronto, Ontario M5A 1J3

This Simon & Schuster Canada edition October 2020

SIMON & SCHUSTER CANADA and colophon are trademarks of Simon & Schuster, Inc.

For information about special discounts for bulk purchases, please contact Simon & Schuster Special Sales
at 1-800-268-3216 or CustomerService@simonandschuster.ca.

Manufactured in the United States of America

10 9 8 7 6 5 4 3 2

Library and Archives Canada Cataloguing in Publication

Title: Past and present / Sarah Richardson.
Names: Richardson, Sarah, 1971- author.
Description: Simon & Schuster Canada edition.
Series statement: Collected ; 2
Identifiers: Canadiana 20200197940 | ISBN 9781982140397 (softcover)
Subjects: LCSH: Interior decoration.
Classification: LCC NK2115 .R53 2020 | DDC 747—dc23

ISBN 978-1-9821-4039-7
ISBN 978-1-9821-4041-0 (ebook)

Editorial Director Beth Hitchcock
Art Director Rose Pereira
Media Manager Jennifer Gibeau
Cover Photography Valerie Wilcox

Collected

BY SARAH RICHARDSON

VOLUME Nº 2

Past + Present

PUBLISHED BY SIMON & SCHUSTER
NEW YORK · LONDON · TORONTO · SYDNEY · NEW DELHI

Contents

PHOTOGRAPHY BY COLIN FAULKNER

WELCOME TO *COLLECTED*, the second volume in my new series designed to engage, inspire, and excite you. This issue dives into the magical alchemy of Past + Present. Ever since I began my career, I've approached every project—whether it's my own home or a client's space—with the goal of creating interiors for modern living that are influenced by a classic perspective. I'm continually inspired by looking back at where we've come from, while optimistically moving toward the future. And so, these pages are packed with as many get-cozy rooms, crave-worthy renovations, and clever designer insights as we could fit in, and I hope they'll help you marry old and new in your own home in a way that makes every day a little more beautiful.

Sarah

OBJECTS OF DESIRE: PAST OR PRESENT?

Our second issue is about finding a balance between old and new, so we asked the people behind the pages: "In your own home, what one thing—whether an object or architectural detail—from either past or present are you most enamored with?"

EDITORIAL TEAM

Above my sofa hang three panels of hand-painted silk in shades of coral, pink, camel, and charcoal by Los Angeles–based wallpaper and textile design firm Porter Teleo. I had them custom made and framed in acrylic boxes, and they bring the living room to life.

BETH HITCHCOCK
Editorial Director

I adore my set of four electric blue and chrome moulded chairs from UK designer Robin Day, circa 1963. I acquired them through a salvage shop for a song. I love a deal, so that just makes me appreciate them even more!

ROSE PEREIRA
Art Director

SRD TEAM

A 1970s heavy glass IITTALA ashtray by Finnish designer Tapio Wirkkala sits on a table in my living room as a decorative bowl, and it's a thing of beauty. The base is impressed with a map of Europe, which to me makes it that much more charming.

JENNIFER GIBEAU
Media Manager,
Sarah Richardson Design

I have a few vintage collections that I love adding to, but I'm quite proud of my purple- and blue-tinted medicine bottles. They look great displayed on their own or arranged with flowers. I even have a few my parents found buried in the backyard of their century home!

CHLOE McPHERSON
Project Assistant,
Sarah Richardson Design

I adore my collection of antique boxes, which I've been collecting since I was a girl. I'm always adding to the collection, which ranges from old Victorian writing boxes to inlaid Syrian boxes. The insides are unique, too—some are lined with old silk, some with paper, and some even have messages inscribed in their lids.

ANNA SPIRO
Designer, "Feeling Blue"

Can I pick one from each? From the past, I have a small crystal chandelier that once hung in my Grandma Zelma's entrance; it's been with me since I owned my first house. In terms of a present-day convenience, I love many things in my home, but when winter comes, I'm grateful we spent the money to install radiant heating under our natural stone floors.

NATALIE HODGINS
Designer, "Fireside Rustic"

The latest thing I'm obsessed with is the woodland-themed wallpaper in our dining room. It's incredibly soothing and magical—especially for a nature lover like myself—and makes me feel like I've stepped into a forest, so it's a wonderful transition to the back patio and our outdoor space.

SUZANNE DIMMA
Designer, "Remaking History"

I have shelves of bins full of objects I've collected over the years. When I want to alter my surroundings, I rummage around and bring a new favourite to the surface. Currently, it's a small brass plate with an embossed skull that I've placed in the library, creating a new tableau that I can enjoy while I read.

COLIN FAULKNER
Photographer, "Remaking History" and "Storybook Victorian"

I wanted my main floor/kitchen renovation to be modern and bright without erasing the home's past. So I kept some of the old architecture, and strategically placed wall sections with window cutouts as room dividers to maintain the feeling of separate rooms while making it just a little more open.

VALERIE WILCOX
Photographer, "Après-Ski? Mais Oui!," "Fireside Rustic," and "Written in the Stars"

My wife and I fell in love with the yard of our 1970s home before we even saw the inside. When we moved in, we realized we'd focused so much on the exterior that we forgot about the carpeted kitchen!

READ McKENDREE
Photographer, "Behind the Dunes"

We just installed an oversized pivot door, and when it's open it allows the outdoors to blend seamlessly into our home and frames a beautiful vista of the ocean for us to appreciate.

KARA ROSENLUND
Photographer, "Feeling Blue"

"THE CLIENT BRIEF WAS TO TURN A CIRCA '80S CHALET NESTLED AT THE BASE OF A SKI HILL INTO A CONTEMPORARY, FAMILY-FRIENDLY WINTER ESCAPE DRESSED IN A SNOW-INSPIRED PALETTE OF PALE GREY, BLUE, AND WHITE."

YES, YOU CAN!

Improve the sightlines by removing acrylic faux mullions from windows.

→ A crowd-pleasing mega-sectional from Sarah's new collection ensures everyone can gather together comfortably. The great room gets an injection of rustic warmth from the unpainted ceiling and a faux antler chandelier that was originally in the dining room, but found new life—and a new location—after a coat of paint.

Après-Ski? Mais Oui!

DESIGN BY SARAH RICHARDSON

PHOTOGRAPHY BY VALERIE WILCOX

DESIGN
BY **SARAH
RICHARDSON**,
SARAH
RICHARDSON
DESIGN

COLLINGWOOD,
ONTARIO

2,250 SQUARE
FEET

34 YEARS OLD

4 BEDROOMS

3 BATHROOMS

14-FOOT
CEILINGS

2 PARENTS,
2 KIDS,
1 PUPPY

2 FIREPLACES

**YES,
YOU CAN!**

If trim's not
special or
significant,
paint it out in
the same colour
as the wall
so it's "barely
there."

S ET AT THE base of a ski resort, this timber-framed chalet was stuck in retro rewind. "We had original 1980s pink and blue tile, laminate counters, Hollywood-style vanity lights—you name it," says designer Sarah Richardson with a laugh. The architecture was just as dominant as the decorating, with pine as far as the eye could see. The owners, a young family with two kids, had always dreamed of a weekend getaway, and Sarah embraced the task. Since she firmly believes design and budget are not mutually exclusive, she dug into the challenge of contemporizing and lightening the entire home while balancing a limited budget with a long renovation checklist. By the time it was complete, no room remained untouched and the chalet was reborn for a new family to begin with an all-new kitchen, three renovated baths, and a top-to-bottom redecoration made possible with endless rolls of new wallpaper, paint, tile, flooring, and furniture throughout.

←

GOOD FROM ANY ANGLE
Swivel chairs allow for ease of conversation when the gang's all there—plus, their solid bases mean you don't see the unfinished underside of a chair when coming up the stairs.

→
Looking to take the stress off a small, high-traffic kitchen? Build a self-serve bar or butler's pantry in an underutilized space. This simple install was done with in-stock cabinetry sprayed in a custom blue hue and dressed up with waterfall quartz counters.

↓
The T-counter offers a blink-and-you'll-miss-it spot to tuck in a pair of counter stools.

"A petite kitchen requires an innovative layout to make it work for entertaining and family life—bisecting the space with a peninsula creates two distinct work zones and delivers maximum counter space!"

—Sarah Richardson

The client mandate was a light and airy space; the
game changer on the upper level was swapping out the
clunky pine railing and surround with a clever in-stock
glass and stainless steel system that delivers sleek
modern style within the timber-framed building.

↓
Chalet living calls for texture! A rattan fixture draws the eye up to the peak of the 14-foot ceilings while a flatweave rug—one of Sarah's designs based on an ages-old batik motif—adds a quiet pattern. Colour is introduced through denim blues that feel soft and comfortable, just the way a ski cabin should.

**Bathroom Wall
Colour:**
Wickham Gray
(HC-171) by
Benjamin Moore
+
**Bedroom
Wall Colour:**
Balboa Mist (OC-27)
by Benjamin Moore

↑
BOLD MOVES

Previously a powder room, this bathroom was expanded for family living. "For a family with young kids, it didn't make sense that the only tub was in the principal bath," says Sarah. "We shrunk the principal ensuite and turned the powder room into a shared bathroom to make the best use of space."

Tongue-and-groove paneling on the walls and a big soaker tub give the bathroom rustic charm and modern style. The mosaic floor tile is based on an antique quilt pattern—a fun reinterpretation of a classic. The vanity was made from inexpensive steel legs, scraps of exterior siding, and a marble remnant.

In the principal bedroom, Sarah sprayed the whole room a soft oyster-toned neutral for a serene effect. The basket light matches the dining room fixture and highlights the high ceilings by casting an organic textured pattern on the ceiling when turned on at night. Tip: Always use a clear bulb with a woven fixture for best effect!

YES, YOU CAN!

Ask your supplier about discontinued materials; this whitewashed oak flooring was a bargain score and transformed the dark and dated interior into a bright and breezy envelope.

↑
The principal bath features a high-low approach with wow-factor results: The vanity was made from in-stock cabinetry (plus budget-friendly lighting and mirrors), but the plumbing fixtures were splurge-worthy.

"Why should a shampoo niche get the spotlight at eye level? Install it lower and within reach to let the fixtures shine instead."

—SR

DETAILS WE LOVE

1- Satin brass hardware feels luxe when contrasted against the white-as-snow palette of the ensuite.

2- A gooseneck-style showerhead is a smart solution when faced with a sloped ceiling and two tall homeowners!

3- Think ahead and ask for an integrated towel hook when having a glass enclosure fabricated.

4- Mosaic wall tiles form a wintery snowflake pattern that shimmers when the sun pours in through the peaked transom window above.

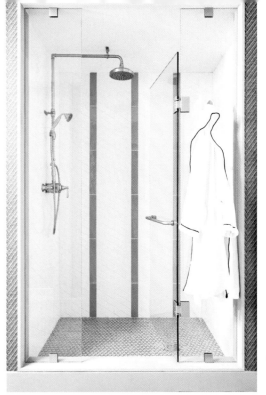

→ Three bands of blue tile add a graphic vertical element to the all-white parallelogram-tiled shower and connect the smoky blue hues used in the bathroom.

↓ "A single off-centred sink is a great way to allow for maximum counter space," says Sarah.

← A self-adhesive mural of birch trees brings the outdoors in with the daughter's favourite palette of blues and greens. The handwoven rattan inset on the headboard and the brass collar accents might not be standard cabin fare but were designed by Sarah as a textural nod to contemporary bedroom style.

APRÈS-SKI? MAIS OUI!

↑
Give basic laminate cupboards a custom touch with inexpensive strips of poplar trim applied to create a chevron pattern. Finish off with paint that echoes the accent colour in the wallpaper and takes the doors beyond basic white.

←
A craft area for the kids—just off both their bedrooms—makes the most of an otherwise unused zone under the stairs and some of the furniture that came with the chalet.

← You can find anything online, including barnboard for cladding walls! A wall-to-wall pine bench was made from a chunky piece of lumber store stock.

← To neutralize an original fieldstone fireplace, the media room was decorated in light tones of cream, sand, oyster, and charcoal.

"The hulking stone fireplace was outfitted with a sleek modern gas insert to create instant coziness after a chilly day in the snow." —SR

"I'VE ALWAYS BEEN DRAWN TO OLD HOUSES FOR THEIR CHARACTER AND HISTORY. EVEN IF THERE ARE QUIRKS AND THE FLOOR SLOPES, THERE'S A BEAUTY TO THAT."

Remaking History

DESIGN BY **SUZANNE DIMMA AND ARRIZ HASSAM**

PHOTOGRAPHY BY **COLIN FAULKNER**

DESIGN BY
SUZANNE DIMMA,
SUZANNE DIMMA DESIGN,
& **ARRIZ HASSAM**,
ARRIZ + CO

TORONTO, ONTARIO

2,500 SQUARE FEET

133 YEARS OLD

8-MONTH RENOVATION

2 BEDROOMS + DEN

2.5 BATHROOMS

11-FOOT CEILINGS

14 NEW BRASS SWITCHPLATES

YES, YOU CAN!

Give yourself permission to marry different woods and finishes together in the same sightline: Suzanne stripped the interior door with a plan to repaint but liked the look of the raw wood beside the console, stool, and floors.

↓
IT'S LIT
Suzanne and Arriz added a Windsor arch insert to the existing mantel to better capture the home's 1887 era.

THE 35TH TIME was the charm. Suzanne Dimma and Arriz Hassam, both designers, were searching for an old house with character they could modernize—the epitome of their shared style. The couple finally found "it" with lucky number 35, a redbrick Victorian in a leafy Toronto neighbourhood known for its village-like cluster of century homes. "The moment I stood on the front porch, which looks out to a park, I was in love," says Suzanne. Inside, the house suffered from a stuck-in-the-'80s floor plan and finishes. With their shared vision, the couple opened up the third floor principal suite, added period-appropriate millwork and paneling throughout, renovated all 2.5 baths, and gave the kitchen a makeover. "Old houses have such warmth, and that's a big part of the appeal," says Suzanne. "When we introduced modern touches that complemented the original character, that's when it truly felt like home—and like us."

"The kitchen was stuck in the '80s but I fell in love with the green marble counters and backsplash, so we decided to keep them." —Suzanne Dimma

DETAILS WE LOVE

1- A rectangular black steel range hood adds gravitas and echoes the black accents in the adjacent living room.

2- A clever layout maximizes light from the front streaming into the kitchen, while the elevated shelf hides all telltale signs of a chef at work.

3- A vintage farm table and rug add texture and soul to the renovated kitchen.

4- The original white oak floor has a unique diagonal pattern and still-visible pegs; it was stripped and oiled for a more current look.

Lower Cabinet Colour:
Marcasite (Q1) by Benjamin Moore
+
Upper Cabinet Colour:
Sea Salt (CSP-95) by Benjamin Moore

←

The rustic farm table in the kitchen
has been with Suzanne for thirty
years; it was the desk in her first
apartment and the dining table in her
first house. Most days now, it's back
to being a desk amidst the hub of the
kitchen. The secret to its longevity?
A classic silhouette and different
paint colours over the years: "Like an
old friend, it's been with me through
lots of changes," she says.

↓

When working with bold natural
stone, select light neutral cabinet
tones to temper the intensity and
create timeless appeal.

↑
A nature lover living in a busy city, Suzanne wanted to feel more connected to the outdoors. This fantastical woodland wallpaper flows from the kitchen's green marble and adds serious wow factor to the petite dining room. Traditional architecture + black modern lighting + a blend of old and new furniture is key to Suzanne and Arriz's curated "past meets present" style.

↓
In a narrow city home on a tree-lined street, more light is always better, and since drapes aren't needed for privacy upstairs, why bother? The open landing acts as Arriz's office and listening room.

↓
A small-scale chair and sconce with a big piece of art in between? Absolutely—simple lines, black accents, and texture make this tight, vertical vignette so eye-catching.

"I call myself a 'Boho Minimalist' because I like layers, but I like them to be clean. I'm always looking for airiness and lightness, and things that can be moved and rearranged. Arriz and I often clear the floor in here and dance!" —SD

Custom built-ins are expensive and you can't take them with you. Here, a store-bought modern Craftsman-style bookshelf accommodates Arriz's record collection and grounds the room's palette of browns, rusts, and charcoals.

YES, YOU CAN!

Have the best of both worlds—smoky glass and warm wood—with two shapely modern tables. Both are small enough to be moved with ease.

←

When you're set on wallpaper in the powder room, be sure to think big on a backsplash to protect your investment. Suzanne and Arriz had this marble slab left over from the counters at their previous house; its dramatic veining looks fresh against the small-scale print and hex tiles. Using a surface-mount sink on the vanity allowed for a lower counter height, making the room feel a tad more spacious. The mini mirror was a flea-market find: "I have a thing for tiny mirrors and art," Suzanne says. "It becomes a curiosity when paired with lots of breathing room."

"The upstairs hallway is the only place we introduced colour on the walls, to act as a transition between public and private spaces and backdrop for art. Painting the trim and doors the same as the wall colour just adds to the drama. Adding a marble top to the niche, where we've displayed a beaded African crown, makes it feel like a special moment."
—SD

Wall Colour:
Hague Blue (30)
by Farrow & Ball

↑

New built-in closets frame the doorway
to a rooftop deck—the perfect spot for
summertime yoga. Applied moulding on the
closet frame and doors gives the millwork a
historic, traditional quality.

↑

A small mid-century modern desk and chair
under the eve makes a perfect perch with a
treetop view for those work-from-home days.

SUITE DREAMS
The third-floor principal bedroom feels like its own apartment. When there's no space for a walk-in closet, built-in wardrobes waste no space yet deliver minimal-chic style, complete with a nook above for dramatic art and lighting, plus a spot for books and glasses.

YES, YOU CAN!
When a wall needs
to be built out to
accommodate
plumbing, turn it
into a beautiful
design feature—
this shelf becomes
a spot for both
pretty and
practical things.

SERENE SANCTUARY

Hand-glazed subway tiles, artisan-made glass sconces, and an antique mirror with patina give the new principal bath some old-world soul. Get maximum counter space with a small, square sink.

A dreamy freestanding tub invites long soaks, while heated, grooved floor tiles feel soothing underfoot. The bathroom's palette of white, cream, and grey—with accents of soft pink—is calming with just a hint of femininity.

"THE DESIGN BRIEF WAS SIMPLE: CREATE A WINTER-ONLY SKI CHALET FOR THREE GENERATIONS OF FAMILY TO GATHER IN COZY-CHIC STYLE THAT'S ANYTHING BUT FUSSY."

—

Fireside Rustic

DESIGN BY NATALIE HODGINS AND SHANNON MORRISON

PHOTOGRAPHY BY VALERIE WILCOX

↑
Stained walls, a new fireplace and mantel, and family-sized seating make the great room a natural gathering spot. Two architectural salvage folk art pieces on the mantel introduce a garnet colour that's used in small doses throughout the chalet. "I think the best way to use red is with restraint," says designer Natalie Hodgins.

DESIGN BY
**NATALIE
HODGINS**
AND **SHANNON
MORRISON**,
SARAH
RICHARDSON
DESIGN

COLLINGWOOD,
ONTARIO

3,000 SQUARE
FEET

30 YEARS OLD

6-MONTH
RENOVATION

4 BEDROOMS

2 BATHROOMS

4 BUNK BEDS

3 GENERATIONS,
4 GRANDKIDS

↓
SNUG AS A BUG
A custom, extra-wide
chaise was designed for
reading sessions with
the grandchildren.

↑
Two 9-foot-long custom sofas ensure everyone gets a seat when the whole family's at the chalet. "I've never done black sofas, but the fabric has a slub through it so it doesn't read as black," says Natalie.

LIKE A SKI race on the nearby hill, this chalet makeover was a sprint to the finish. The clients—a couple with two grown children and four grandchildren—bought the chalet in July and needed it weekend-ready by November. "I've worked with these clients before and when they ask, I accept the challenge and deliver," says designer Natalie Hodgins. The first uphill battle? Minimizing the knotty pine that covered the walls and ceilings of the early 1980s building. "Our painter came up with some clever colours and treatments, so rather than replace or cover the pine—because no one wants drywall in a chalet—we sandblasted and restained the walls and painted the trim," says Natalie. With that transformation complete, the kitchen and bathrooms were renovated, and the entire place furnished to suit the whole family. Decorating a winter-use-only space means all the fabrics were selected for their winter-cozy touchability (like chenille and cashmere), and most are washable. "Nothing's too precious," says Natalie. "It's the perfect family getaway for a snowy weekend or week away."

The chalet's owners may be grandparents, but they embrace bold design. The flexibility offered by designing a winter-only space meant the use of a richer, deeper palette of graphite, charcoal, and smoke brought to life with layered textures and patterns to deliver monochromatic interest.

FINE LINES ↓
Horizontal tongue and groove mixes with a vertically reeded bedside table and Nordic-inspired striped fabric for an intersection of perpendicular elements.

Both of the homeowners' two grown children get their own sink and storage to share with their respective spouses and children in the high-traffic shared bathroom.

④

DETAILS WE LOVE

1- Oil-rubbed bronze sconces finished with a rope wrap—a riff on vintage oil lamps— add to the rustic cabin-chic vibe.

2- Porcelain tiles installed in a chevron pattern reinforce the snow-inspired neutral palette used throughout the chalet.

3- Durable, wood-patterned melamine cabinets and a Caesarstone top mean the vanity won't chip, scratch, or fade.

4- Elongated hexagonal mirrors with beveled glass were custom made for a one-of-a-kind touch.

"We took a nautically inspired approach to efficient use of space, with extra-narrow side tables and surface-saving, wall-mounted sconces—now it's a comfy place to tuck in."

—Natalie Hodgins

↑
Wintry artwork and pillows with a snowflake motif add subtle flair to a bedroom that's rich in texture but short on square footage.

→
The bunk room has four beds, each with built-in storage nook and reading light. Natalie bought three multipiece frame sets to create an instant gallery that's easy to change up and expand as the memories grow over the years.

"OUR GOAL FOR THIS CLASSIC SHINGLED NANTUCKET HOME WAS TO DELIVER A COASTAL FEELING THAT BROUGHT IN SHADES OF BLUE IN A VERY THOUGHTFUL, TONED-DOWN WAY, MAKING IT STYLISH BUT COMFORTABLE FOR A YOUNG FAMILY."

Ocean-blue shutters look fresh against the home's weathered cedar shake shingles.

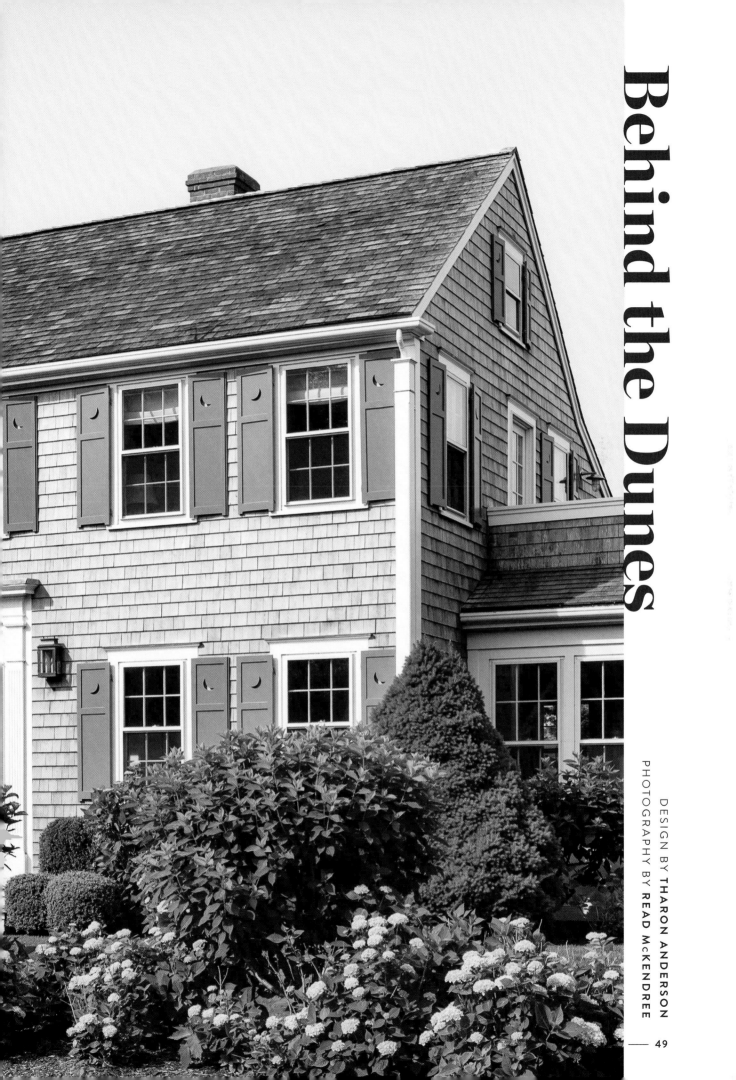

Behind the Dunes

DESIGN BY **THARON ANDERSON**

PHOTOGRAPHY BY **READ McKENDREE**

— 49

DESIGN BY
**THARON
ANDERSON**,
THARON
ANDERSON
DESIGN

NANTUCKET, MA.

5,000 SQUARE
FEET

90 YEARS OLD

4 BEDROOMS

4.5 BATHROOMS

1 POOL HOUSE

15 COATS OF
FLOOR PAINT

5 MINUTES TO
THE OCEAN

YES, YOU CAN!
Put a classic decorator shirred
fabric shade on a mod lamp base.

←

NATURAL BEAUTY

A turned-leg table wrapped in rope anchors an airy hallway vignette. Handpainted grasscloth wallpaper adds a playful element, while a gesso mirror offers a nod to an oyster shell.

→

In a corner of the living room, light streams in from an uncovered window—it's the perfect spot to place some oversized flowering branches that almost seem to be climbing the wall.

IT TAKES ONE islander to truly understand another. So when it came time for the owners of this shingled Colonial, a young family from Connecticut, to refresh their summer home, the wife—who grew up on Nantucket—called on New York–based designer Tharon Anderson, also a Nantucket native. The bones of the home, just a short walk away from a quiet tidal beach, were already in good shape. What it needed most was a makeover: "Once I met the wife, it was easy to take my cues from her style," says Tharon. "She always looks fresh and unfussy even when she's wearing a pair of jeans." The biggest transformation was painting out the home's existing floors: It took fifteen coats of sealant and paint to ensure the reddish-toned mahogany wouldn't show through. The work—and the risk—was worth it. "Because it's an older home, the ceilings are relatively low and this change brightened everything up," says Tharon. Beachy white floors created the perfect blank canvas for neutral fabrics, woven textures, and wallpaper, all with just a kiss of blue from the nearby ocean. Now, the look is Nantucket chic without any of the nautical clichés.

↑
Ivory grasscloth wallpaper, uncovered windows, and neutral furniture—a mix of printed linen upholstery and cotton slipcovers—give the living room unfussed coastal charm with seaside sophistication.

← An indoor/outdoor awning-striped runner in white and taupe adds dimension to the all-white kitchen and can be thrown in the wash for an easy clean—a must at a beach house.

↓ Painting the handrail and treads the same colour as the floors makes the narrow staircase feel wider and keeps the focus on the wallpaper.

"Most coastal homes are nautical with deep blues, and that was never our direction. Instead, we used seafoam and aqua to bring in those watery swimming-pool tones that feel newer and fresher."

—Tharon Anderson

← Blink and you'll almost miss the beach theme, from the modern woven rush chairs to the plaster chandelier that looks like a cross between coral and a piece of driftwood. A hint of seafoam comes into play thanks to artwork and a small-scale print on the drapes.

DETAILS WE LOVE

1- When white linen shades meet white walls, the eye is drawn out to the main event: lush greenery and views of the harbour.

2- V-groove paneling applied to follow the profile of a tray ceiling enhances the architectural interest and beachy mood.

3- A bleached jute area rug allows just a hint of the painted floors to show at the room's perimeter. "I don't believe in wall-to-wall carpet in a beach house," says Tharon.

4- An upholstered bed with matching bedskirt is the patterned counterpoint to a room outfitted with spare furnishings and streamlined designed.

→
SERENITY NOW

A modern gesso lamp and lacquered Parsons side table show stunning restraint against petite floral upholstery in the principal bedroom.

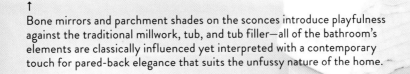

↑
Bone mirrors and parchment shades on the sconces introduce playfulness against the traditional millwork, tub, and tub filler—all of the bathroom's elements are classically influenced yet interpreted with a contemporary touch for pared-back elegance that suits the unfussy nature of the home.

YES, YOU CAN!
Add extra-wide shiplap to drywall for calming, beach-house vibes wherever you are.

↑
In the daughter's bedroom, the same blue unifies two different prints by wallpaper and textile designer Lulie Wallace—a smart way to create a cohesive look without being matchy.

TWIN POWER
The softness of fully upholstered bedframes offset the hard lines of the wood paneling. "I design rooms that can grow with children," says Tharon. "The idea is that even guests could be comfortable in here."

"The pool is a family gathering spot for swimming, playing games, and hosting cookouts, so plenty of seating was essential. These outdoor wicker loungers can be easily hosed down and are visually lighter than the teak furniture commonly used on Nantucket." —TA

GREEN ACRES

With doors wide open, the pool house becomes a symmetrical extension of the outdoor living space. Stone pavers mirror the weathered shingles of the pool house's exterior, allowing the lush lawn, trees, and hedges to pull focus.

PRIVACY, PLEASE!

A stone retaining wall and symmetrical planters draw the eye up to a white moon gate—a Nantucket classic—flanked by a manicured privet hedge.

"If you're seeking respite from the sun, what better place to lie down than in an indoor/outdoor living room? We kept the pool house casual to match the main house, but furnished it inexpensively with in-stock and ready-made furniture and upholstery; nothing is custom or precious when wet bathing suits are around!" —TA

BE OUR GUEST

A compact but fully functional kitchen makes it easy to grab drinks and prepare lunches in wet bathing suits without going in the main house. A palette of pale aquas and bright blues is pulled from the pool itself.

→

The pool house bedroom was envisioned as a dreamy destination. Shiplap walls and a tester bed add to the crisp-yet-cozy factor.

CALDERA
HOUSE HOTEL

12 WAYS
TO USE BLUE

7 CRAVE-WORTHY
BUNK BEDS

4 FABULOUS
VANITIES

Global Edit

Our roundup of what's new (and old!), celebrating the most swoon-worthy past and present styles from around the world.

GETAWAY GOALS

ROOMS WITH A VIEW

There's plenty of inspiration at Jackson Hole's Caldera House, whether your vacation is real or virtual.

—

calderahouse.com

A red rug feels right when all the other furniture is neutral, while an off-centred hearth is an unexpectedly cool detail.

Each suite has its own spacious balcony, making it easy to host a mountain-view feast for family and friends.

IF EVER A PLACE made us declare, "I want to go to there," it's the Caldera House boutique hotel. The über-chic chalet—nestled into the base of the Teton mountain range in Jackson Hole, Wyoming—puts a modern spin on "cabin fever." Sleek two- and four-bedroom suites are like a home away from home with chef's kitchens and generous living spaces. The hotel's interiors also come with serious cred: It was designed by award-winning studios Commune Design and Carney Logan Burke. At cozy Caldera House, the skiing is epic but the après-ski scene is even better!

Blond oak floors and ceilings are a Scandi-perfect canvas for sexy, low-slung furniture in shades of cognac, tan, and pine. Multiple multi-armed fixtures cover the ceiling like a constellation of stars.

Though the silhouette of this soaker tub is traditional, the contemporary niche and floor-mount taps are anything but. A super-soft sheepskin rug makes stepping out of this deep tub just as dreamy as stepping in.

YES, YOU CAN!
Float a piece of live-edge wood above a mattress for a rustic headboard.

Roll out of bed and into your ski gear—the Jackson Hole Mountain Resort tram is literally outside your door.

Dark flagstone floors and raw wood walls create dramatic sauna chic.

Two ideas we love in this eat-in kitchen? An island with stepped levels and pedestal base for max dining occupancy, plus pantry doors with hidden hardware that blend in with the wood-clad wall.

FEELING BLUE

Do you love blue like we do? Here's a roundup of 12 brilliant blue ideas from Brisbane, Australia, designer Anna Spiro, who deftly mixes fresh with fearless.

PHOTOGRAPHY BY KARA ROSENLUND

LET THE FLOOR STEAL THE SHOW

One big brushstroke of blue goes a long way, so when the tiles are this spectacular, keep the rest of the fixtures white to keep all eyes on the floor.

USE IT IN
SMALL DOSES
Take your pattern play to a whole new expert level with the Anna Approach. Leafy chocolate-brown wallpaper is the backdrop that anchors a mixed gallery wall, and a painterly patterned blue lampshade adds extra punch to the vignette.

↑
BRING IN BLUE WITH ART

Make the most of your flea-market finds and create a gallery portrait wall by mixing and matching vintage paintings in various frames for a dramatic statement.

UPHOLSTER THE WALLS

One-hue rooms work best when you mix a variety of patterns and print sizes: Solid walls are paired with a mini-print lumbar pillow and a medium-sized floral on the headboard.

COLOUR BLOCK YOUR BOOKS

Up your #shelfie game by letting one theme colour dominate and alternating books in vertical and horizontal blocks to create organization with a nod to pattern play.

LET BLUE PLAY NICELY WITH OTHERS

In a multihued room, other colours have their moment (hello, orange sofa!) but blue is the constant thread from the floor up.
PHOTOGRAPHY BY TIM SALISBURY

EYE SPY

Sarah Richardson for Kravet Decowaves Fabric in Jade

LIGHTEN UP

Anna gives a master class in mixing prints with sky blue and navy as the dominant duo. When playing with pattern, be sure to inject some solid colours to break up all the activity.

PHOTOGRAPHY BY TIM SALISBURY

EMBRACE YOUR MOOD INDIGO

Cobalt and royal blue have strength when used at the same saturation.

EYE SPY

What does every picture on this page have in common? Patterned lampshades! Why would you ever go back to basic white?

1

2

3

4

DETAILS WE LOVE

1- At Paper Daisy restaurant on Australia's east coast, Ikat shades put a fun twist on a traditional triple-armed sconce.

2- A salvaged mirror with beautifully chipped blue paint adds just the right touch of patina.

3- No need to be too precious about hanging vintage plates—keep the arrangement loose.

4- Woven, bistro-style seating and striped pillows are ever-fresh together.

BUNKING IN

Cute? Check. Cozy? Check. So irresistible that even grown-ups will want to crawl in? You bet! Here's how seven savvy designers did it right.

CHIC & COZY

Smoky green paint, a playful wallpapered ceiling, and built-in cubbies give these bunks, dreamed up by Los Angeles designer Dee Murphy, adult appeal. Why should kids get all the fun?

PHOTOGRAPHY BY ZEKE RUELAS

→ OPPOSITES ATTRACT

In a weekend house designed for welcoming crowds, this max occupancy bunk room was born from leftover building materials. Sarah Richardson used bits of extra lumber, and the original construction stairs were reimagined and put to good use in this sunny built-in bunk room.

PHOTOGRAPHY BY STACEY BRANDFORD

↑ SHIP SHAPE

A nautical palette and fun chevron floor make this bunk room by Charleston, South Carolina, designer Jenny Keenan feel yacht-worthy. Individual grommeted curtains say, "Privacy, please!"

PHOTOGRAPHY BY JULIA LYNN

↓ SMALL BUT MIGHTY

When is a playhouse not a playhouse? When it's also a double-decker bed. Salt Lake City, Utah, firm Ashton Klomp Interiors took advantage of a tight squeeze to fit in two kid-sized bunks, though the blue-grey paint, plaid rug, and striped ceiling give the space enough maturity to grow with junior.

PHOTOGRAPHY BY CHRIS LUKER

GLOBAL EDIT

↑

RESTFUL RESTRAINT

In a modern Whistler, British Columbia, ski chalet, designer Sophie Burke stuck to a pared-back Scandi palette. Extra-wide solid oak tongue-and-groove walls installed horizontally give a crisp modern edge to this bunk room, delivering a result that blends elegance with practical durability thanks to the solid-wood construction.
PHOTOGRAPHY BY EMA PETER

←

OUT OF AFRICA

Designer Heather Chadduck of Birmingham, Alabama, used ceiling-height curtains with a tasseled leading edge, tiger prints, and a woven rug to transform these sleeping quarters into a glam safari camp.

PRETTY IN PINK

X marks the spot—or the railing, in this case—of these sweet, blush-pink bunks. Layered up with chenille spreads and plush pillows, the room, designed by Sydney, Australia's, Three Birds Renovations, artfully blends pretty details with DIY projects and budget finds. PHOTOGRAPHY BY CHRIS WARNES

YES, YOU CAN!

Make simple builder-grade wood look like custom cabinetry with applied moulding on walls and out-of-the-box thinking on functional elements like railings.

VANITY FLAIR

In the eyes of Sarah Richardson, a vanity is never just a counter or storage spot; it's an opportunity for the three Rs—reduce, reuse, recycle—in the most stylish and surprising ways.

CHARACTER BUILDING

A piece of 1800s wainscoting with a bump out became the foundation for a countertop and backsplash that mimic the profile of architectural salvage. The mirror is created from a pair of antique Egyptian windows.

PHOTOGRAPHY BY VALERIE WILCOX

Wall Colour: Silver Cloud (30YY 63/024) by Glidden

GROOVY IDEA

Dig the vibes of teak furniture but not the colour? Sarah painted a '60s credenza with grooved panels and added round glass and chrome hardware for a look that's more modern than mid-century.

PHOTOGRAPHY BY STACEY BRANDFORD

Wall Colour: Ethereal Blue (90BG 72/038) by CIL

FARM FRESH

Leftover barn beams serve as the solid support for an extra-wide guest room vanity crafted on-site. The wood's rough-hewn patina acts as a country counterpoint to glossy blue subway tiles.

PHOTOGRAPHY BY STACEY BRANDFORD

Wall Colour: Snowfield White (00NN 72/000) by Glidden

DESK JOB

No homework necessary when an antique pine desk becomes an unexpected vanity with a marble-remnant counter and round surface-mount sink.

PHOTOGRAPHY BY STACEY BRANDFORD

Wall Colour: Forest Light (30GY 83/064) by Dulux

BETHANIE LYALL   MISCHA COUVRETTE

JOHN WARD   ÉLAINE FORTIN

DAVID SCHONBERGER   NINA TOLSTRUP

Into the Woods

Not just for floors, trim, or furnishings, wood is a renewable resource with texture and tactile beauty—a soft-to-the-touch material that's a durable and adaptable starting point for a multitude of makers, turning a living material into something soulful and artful for your home.

BETHANIE LYALL

Bethanie Kaye Design
Furniture | Sculpture | Utensils
BETHANIEKAYE.COM

CREATIVE PROCESS

I believe in taking something that otherwise would have wound up in a landfill or a fire and turning it into functional art for your home. Inspiration comes from everywhere— my family, the lampshade at a diner, the way water has washed over stones and driftwood. Sometimes I'll even see a piece of clothing that gives me an idea on how to form my next piece.

TRAINING GROUND

I come from a long line of female artists: My mom was a stained glass artist, her sister is a ceramicist, and their mother, my grandmother, was a landscape painter. I've always been drawn to working with my hands. I've made jewellery, studied ceramics, and eventually taught myself how to turn wood by using an old lathe and even older chisels.

WOOD OF CHOICE

I love working with iroko. It turns beautifully, and once the piece is oiled you're left with an incredible amber colour that fits in with any style of decor and looks incredible alongside other species of wood.

PRICE RANGE

From $30 for candleholders to $1,800 for 72" high sculptures.

FROM TOP
Bowls, $55-$300

—

Spoons, from $80

—

Table, $1,100

—

Vases, $85-$300

—

Candlesticks, $60-$140

JOHN WARD

Treeware Woodworks
Candlesticks | Vessels | Trays
TREEWARE.CA

CREATIVE PROCESS

Trying to translate a visualized shape with a chisel and a piece of wood spinning at 2500 rpm.

TRAINING GROUND

I'm a refugee from corporate IT, and a self-taught hobbyist turned full-time woodworker. But wood turning isn't really work! It's the sanding that's a drag.

WOOD OF CHOICE

My favourite is the one on the lathe. I'm not being facetious; each type of wood is different and you have to appreciate its unique qualities or you won't be successful in your turning. That said, I spend 90% of my time with white ash—not the easiest wood to work but always a pleasure in the end.

PRICE RANGE

From $85 to $110 for candlesticks.

Turned candlesticks
from $85 to $110

RIGHT
Black walnut board,
$225-$325
—
BELOW
White ash board,
$135-$155

DAVID SCHONBERGER

Ottercreek Woodworks
Charcuterie boards
OTTERCREEKWOODWORKS.COM

INTENTION
I want people to feel a connection to nature, and a respect for trees and the integral role forests play in the health of our planet. I also hope my boards will offer more opportunity for families to sit down and eat together, to share conversation and keep family traditions alive.

WOOD OF CHOICE
White oak. Great sailing ships, timber-framed structures, fine furniture, and even whisky barrels are made from oak—when I'm working with it, I often imagine the smells and sounds of a shipyard of times gone by.

ONE COOL FACT
I offer an award-winning culinary experience called "From Tree to Table: A Build-Your-Own Board Experience" hosted in my woodshop. It gives guests an opportunity to Forest Breathe, create your own live-edge charcuterie board with locally harvested lumber, and indulge in a handpicked selection of local charcuterie, cheeses, preserves, and breads.

PRICE RANGE
From $35 (14" length) to $875 (72" length).

LEFT
Oldtown Stool in
walnut and white
oak, from $2,274
—
BELOW
Junction Table
Light in white oak
with natural finish,
$854

MISCHA COUVRETTE

hollis+morris
Lighting | Furniture | Accessories
HOLLISANDMORRIS.COM

TRAINING GROUND

I rely heavily on intuition. After studying
marine biology and environmental
sciences, I refurbished a steel sailboat
with some friends and we sailed to
Guatemala. The experience sparked
my interest in building and design;
something that looks great but doesn't
function will do you no good at sea!

WOOD OF CHOICE

We work with white oak and walnut,
which we can source locally. I love the
variation and richness of walnut, but
you can't overlook the dense and reliable
form of white oak.

INSPIRATION

I've always believed that less is more—
if you can distill a design to its core you
have the highest chance of reaching the
most people. The more essential the
form, the more opportunity there is for
it to spark a subjective experience and
authentic inspiration.

PRICE RANGE

From $150 for trays to $7,850 for dining
tables.

FROM OUR FRIENDS AT FOGO

Surrounded by sea and salt air, The Woodshop on Fogo Island, Newfoundland, is a creative hub for makers from all over the world—and their pieces tell a story of place. That was founder Zita Cobb's mandate: to honour the Islanders who came before through what she describes as "handmade modern" objects that deliver joy and meaning along with form and function. As an initiative to help secure a thriving future for Fogo, informative "Economic Nutrition" labels on all products tell you where your money goes—and how it'll be invested back into the local community. Do good while buying great goods? It's a win-win for everybody.

CHIC SPLURGE

The Punt Chair, designed by Montreal's Élaine Fortin and found in many of the Fogo Island Hotel's guest rooms, is made from tamarack or spruce, and takes inspiration from the structural ribs of small wooden fishing boats.

GREAT VALUE

Made from off-cuts of yellow birch, UK-based designer Nina Tolstrup's doorstop resembles a traditional saltbox house—a fun detail in a piece not normally designed to be eye-catching. Hang from the leather cord when not in use.

ZITA COBB
Creator and CEO
SHOREFAST.COM

RIGHT
Punt Chair in tamarack or spruce, $5,900

—
BELOW
Doorstop, $40

"WORKING ON A HOME WITH AS MUCH HISTORY AS THIS ONE WAS DEEPLY EXCITING. THOUGH IT HAD A LOT OF ARCHITECTURAL CHARACTER, OUR CLIENTS, A YOUNG FAMILY, WANTED THE INTERIORS TO FEEL MORE CONTEMPORARY, CASUAL, AND KID-FRIENDLY."

Old Soul, New Start

↓
Wow moments happen when a historic home's original features get new life thanks to the addition of modern art and furniture. The magic is in the mix: Restored beams and trim look crisp covered in high-gloss paint, while two comfy streamlined sectionals—and cube ottomans—offer up plenty of soft places for a busy family with two young sons to sprawl, nap, and play.

Wall + Trim Colour:
Shoreline (1471) by Benjamin Moore

DESIGN BY **SUSANA SIMONPIETRI**
PHOTOGRAPHY BY **SARAH ELLIOTT**

87

DESIGN BY
**SUSANA
SIMONPIETRI**,
CHANGO & CO.

WESTPORT,
CONNECTICUT

8,000 SQUARE
FEET

217 YEARS OLD

6-MONTH
RENOVATION

7 BEDROOMS

8 BATHROOMS

2 PARENTS,
2 KIDS

160-FOOT
RELOCATION

↓
YOUTHFUL GLOW
Respect the past but bring it into the
present—that's a winning recipe for updating
an old house without erasing its charm. Here,
the entry hall's enveloped in high-gloss white
paint that shines like glass when exposed to
natural light. Sleek touches, like a sculptural
lamp with drum shade, a modern console, and
oversized round mirror, make the architecture
less fussy and formal.

→

The look of gorgeously styled shelves says "effortless," but there's plenty of thought behind the process. Five secrets for success:

1- Keep the colour palette restrained (unless you're going for a colour-blocked approach).

2- Choose a mix of objects like books, baskets, art, and found objects.

3- Dip into your collections to find an item that can take the lead as a recurring motif (like the white pottery pictured here).

4- Play with scale, levels, and texture so each shelf has a unique arrangement, variety of heights, and combination of materials to engage the eye.

5- Don't be afraid to embrace negative space. Sometimes one perfect thing is more than enough.

R **ELOCATION IS THE** buzzword for this house: Not only did the homeowners, a family of four with two young boys, move from the city to the countryside of Westport, Connecticut, but their house moved, too. The 1803 historic home was restored by a local builder and architect with a passion for preservation and, in the process, the entire home was picked up from its original location near the road and moved back 60 feet to take better advantage of the wide-open countryside setting. "The builder and architect chose to restore the original beams and wide-plank floors, so the bones of the house were already quite minimal and refined when we came on the scene," says designer Susana Simonpietri. "Those elements set the tone. The biggest change we made was adding contrast with contemporary furniture, sculptural accessories, and infusing bright oranges and yellows throughout the home to make it relaxed and inviting for both family time and hosting." With their dream home complete, it's safe to say this family won't be relocating again—they're here to stay.

DETAILS WE LOVE

1- Take a range hood from an appliance to a design feature by running a stainless band between two cabinets, restaurant-style.

2- Make a traditional frame-style kitchen (complete with crown moulding) seem fresh and new with restrained slab door fronts and streamlined hardware.

3- Globe pendants are an airy modern twist on the traditional lantern silhouette.

4- Who says you need a row of uppers? English-style cabinets that sit atop the counters provide useful open storage but keep the kitchen feeling airy.

3

Wall Colour: Decorator's White (CC-20) by Benjamin Moore

4

"Serene, chic, and clean—is there a more stylish mandate for a principal bedroom?"
—Susana Simonpietri

↑
Got an angled roofline? Embrace your architectural elements, and add drama (and the effect of a higher ceiling) by mounting a trio of art above a low-slung headboard. The symmetry of matching bedside tables and lamps adds visual calm and tranquility.

↓
What could be dreamier than a glam vanity table bathed in natural light and dressed in nothing but hushed tones of cream on oyster on alabaster, with touchable accents of nubbly bouclé?

←

TRANQUIL TONES

In a guest room, a sleek yet streamlined sofa tucked under a dormer window is accented with a mod, sculptural black side table that slides as needed to be a convenient perch for a laptop or cup of tea.

↓

The view from the bed is this beauty of a gallery wall above a whitewashed country-style console. Sticking with a strict palette of creams, whites, and blacks is a foolproof formula for sophistication—it just works. Susana mixed line drawings and abstract modern art to make the gallery wall cohesive.

A double-ended slipper tub lets you take in leafy views from either side, the ultimate in forest bathing. Shimmering walls of tile—a classic look to suit the home's vintage—get a boost of modern flavour from rustic yet refined accessories to bring the energy of the outdoors in.

The homeowners had a baby on the way as the house was being designed, so Susana pulled out all the stops. Places to sit, sleep, and put things up (like feet) or down (like a mug) are key for new moms. Steel-blue starry wallpaper wraps up the walls and dormer ceiling, while pale grey trim provides a hint of grounding contrast. When it comes to nursery furniture, think long-term: a Scandi-chic leather rocking chair can come to play in another room once baby grows up.

"As a motif, stars are clean yet playful. We think of children as such dreamers, so why not fill their spaces and their eyes with stars?" –ss

↓
You can't go wrong with an all-white bath—it's an enduring classic. But you can add fun and daring elements, like playful pop art, brilliant dandelion-yellow towels, and graphic wallpaper with a barely there print that adds energy without a busy pattern.

↑
In the four-year-old boy's room, open shelving keeps toys and puzzles close at hand while a soft, chunky woven rug invites on-the-spot play.

INTO THE BLUE

For a colourful bedding mix, start with a fun, inexpensive sheet set and throw blanket, then layer in a higher-end bedspread or quilt, and pillows with colour and personality to polish it off. "This process gives us a license for online shopping and idea-hunting, and results in a mix of different brands, but it's the best way to create something truly unique," says Susana.

Nothing adds interest, texture, and dimension like wallpaper—and there are many options that are anything but flat. This one, inspired by the craft of Berber artisans in Morocco, features a white woven textile laminated against a blue background, resulting in the look and feel of well-loved denim.

"The mandate for designing a forever home to grow with a young family? Make the big elements like wallpaper and large furniture pieces transitional, and be bold, sporty, and cool with colour and finishing touches." –ss

"WHEN GIVEN THE CHANCE TO BUILD A HOUSE FROM
THE GROUND UP, WE WANTED TO CREATE A FOREVER
FARMHOUSE THAT WOULD FEEL AS THOUGH IT BELONGED
ON THE LAND AND ITS SURROUNDINGS, AND WOULD STAND
THE TEST OF TIME, BOTH IN MATERIALS AND DESIGN, WHILE
BEING FULLY OFF THE GRID—THAT'S A TALL ORDER!"

PHOTOGRAPHY BY ALEX MOLE

Written in the Stars

DESIGN BY SARAH RICHARDSON

PHOTOGRAPHY BY STACEY BRANDFORD AND VALERIE WILCOX

↑
Sarah and her husband, Alexander, spent years thinking about and researching the design of their country home on a remote 100-acre property reached by a winding (and steep) kilometre-long driveway. The building is set on a north/south axis to take full advantage of the expansive escarpment views (and show-stopping sunsets). The new home embraces historic architectural details like a porte cochere (to keep the snow off the cars in winter), a belvedere (for enjoying the 360-degree views), and a single-storey sunroom (to reflect the style of century farmhouses that had been added onto over the decades).

DESIGN BY
SARAH RICHARDSON,
SARAH RICHARDSON DESIGN

CREEMORE, ONTARIO

7,000 SQUARE FEET

3 YEARS OLD

9-MONTH RENOVATION

5 BEDROOMS

4.5 BATHROOMS

97 NEW WINDOWS

72 SOLAR PANELS

1 TV SERIES

61 STAIRS FROM TOP TO BOTTOM

←
Off the entry foyer is a raised landing with a pair of vintage Os de Mouton chairs bought at a consignment shop and reupholstered in a casual check. To add to the sculptural silhouette, Sarah embellished with brush fringe instead of piping. A pair of antique columns from a salvage shop and an exterior lantern cum pendant fixture set the tone for a new house filled with plenty of old treasures.

SOMETIMES, YOU HAVE to follow where the road takes you. For Sarah and her husband, Alexander Younger, that happened while bouncing along in an old convertible and admiring the fall colours on a sunny October afternoon. They happened upon a road they'd never travelled before—and it changed the course of their family history. Within a week, they'd taken their two daughters on a hike to explore the overgrown trails on the 100-acre property and fallen in love with its privacy and magnificent views of the Niagara Escarpment. Soon, a deal was signed, the property purchased, and the dream of their forever house was born. Sarah and Alexander spend city life in a sleek, mid-century home, so the goal for their country life was a home with the charm and character of historic houses they admired, but all the modern conveniences and wide-open spaces to suit their lifestyle. "Every room was designed for entertaining and gathering," says Sarah. "The dining table is thirteen feet long and still doesn't always hold all the guests!" Named for the dark night sky, Starlight Farm was realized in record time—a nine-month marathon of side-by-side work and investment for the husband and wife duo, who shared the entire experience on their HGTV series, *Sarah Off the Grid*.

PHOTOGRAPHY BY STACEY BRANDFORD

The sunroom was a last-minute "Do we do it?" But Sarah generally takes an "If in doubt, do!" approach to life and added it to the architectural plan. As a single-storey bump out on the north side of the building, this quietly cozy lounge is a favourite getaway room no matter the season.

When the view is the main entertainment, make windows as tall as you can. Adding a transom to the top of single hung windows adds extra cloud-viewing benefits.

The living room is sunken to create a high-ceilinged gathering space as the anchor of the main floor. The adjacent raised area makes an impromptu stage/dance platform when entertaining. No space should take itself too seriously—and every country room should beckon with lots of options for laid-back weekend living and lounging. With the goal of designing a house filled with timeless, never-tire-of-it interiors, Sarah relied on all-natural and all-neutral fabrics for the living room.

↑
Where does the vision for a home begin? For Starlight Farm, the kitchen was ground zero for the overall house design. When starting with a new house plan, know what you want for the best end result—the brief for this kitchen included a sun-filled kitchen window banquette and table, a 10-foot-plus island, loads of counter space, a bar, and a fireside gathering area with comfy chairs flanking a woodstove for chilly mornings and pre-dinner chats. With these features in mind, the layout of this space informed the rest of the floor plan within the symmetrical architectural plan.

PHOTOGRAPHY BY STACEY BRANDFORD

↓ In a cool-hued kitchen defined by soft grey-paneled cabinetry and 10-foot-high ceilings, brass accents in the form of domed pendants, cabinet hardware, and brass panel insets add a glint of warmth.

YES, YOU CAN!

Looking to install lovely floors and keep your eye on the bottom line? Sarah favours sanded-on-site "character grade" white oak floors—the wood is less expensive than "select and better" grade due to knots and colour variations, but when working with natural materials, character is where it's at!

↓
The view from the front door is down the length of the dining table and out the doors across the distant horizon, so the table was an important anchor to the sparely decorated room. Custom made from salvaged barn floorboards and based on an eighteenth-century Flemish design (with a star motif as a whimsical nod to Starlight Farm), the table is surrounded with rattan chairs to ensure that dinner parties are the epitome of casual, laid-back luxe.

PHOTOGRAPHY BY VALERIE WILCOX (TOP AND BOTTOM LEFT) / STACEY BRANDFORD (TOP AND BOTTOM RIGHT)

GAME ON

(*Above left*) When space permits, consider adding a multifunctional table and chairs to the living room mix. A pair of caned chairs with upholstered seats make the ideal spot for board games, cards, puzzling—or an impromptu spot for working on a laptop.

FIRE'S BURNING

(*Below left*) A "signature Sarah" decor move is to ensure there's always a pair of chairs cozied up to the fireplace. Fireside chats are so much better when you can feel the heat radiating. A petite pair of vintage tub chairs offer wraparound comfort in a small-scale dose!

TETE À TETE

(*Above right*) The house was designed with big bay windows to create the feeling of being connected to the outdoors while cozied up inside. A pair of high-back linen wing chairs are a popular destination for a cup of coffee or a glass of wine.

DREAMY DUO

(*Below right*) From the early days, Sarah always imagined a pair of lounge chairs tucked into the principal bedroom bay window as a quiet spot to daydream and watch the clouds float by. When placing chairs opposite each other, select a shapely silhouette that's pleasing from all angles.

DETAILS WE LOVE

1- The bathroom was designed to draw in maximum views while soaking. The sleek profile of the bathtub acts as a contemporary counterpoint to the classically inspired vanities.

2- To play up the length of the bathroom and create a visual pathway to the views outside, Sarah designed a Carrara marble "carpet" within the floor using four different shapes and sizes of tile. Measure this idea more than once before you install to guarantee stellar results!

3- Instead of the de rigeur vanity sconce, Sarah often prefers to mix up the lighting choices in a bathroom. Vintage milk glass shades were turned into pendants and a single vintage Italian decorative sconce takes centre stage on the wall.

4- His and hers vanities are connected by a recessed vanity table with a shearling-covered stool as a perch. The millwork blends a diamond-patterned door with narrower than usual shaker cabinetry fronts for a then-and-now blend with a historic nod.

↓

The recipe for adding some past-inspired character to a modern-day build? A carved fragment from a church was given a fresh paint treatment and dressed in handkerchief linen panels to frame a contemporary upholstered headboard, while an antique carved mahogany settee was sprayed in grey lacquer and upholstered in matching cream chenille. Modern accents in the form of side tables, lamps, and a graphic rug round out the mix.

"Hallways and landings aren't just circulation spaces to pass through on your way to a more important destination, in my view. They should interest you, intrigue you, and make you pause to soak in every little detail." –SR

↑
Softly textured wallpaper, an elegant console table, a grouping of landscape paintings, and a few special accents is a welcome greeting when you reach the top of the stairs.

←
STEP RIGHT UP

This narrow staircase leads to the above-the-trees belvedere lookout. The glossy aqua-painted stairs turned out to be a happy accident. When they showed up in the wrong wood species (maple instead of oak to match the floors throughout), Sarah decided to move full steam ahead and install them, then chose a cheery colour to give them a nod to easy cottage style.

PHOTOGRAPHY BY VALERIE WILCOX

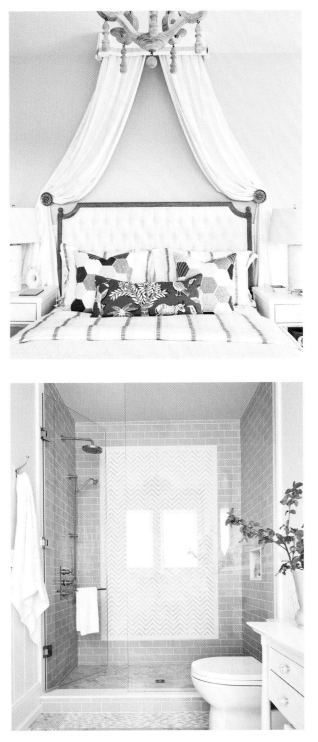

CHIC CANOPY

(Above left) When one daughter asked for a canopy, Sarah figured out how to create it using drapery cotton embellished with grosgrain ribbon that's anchored around vintage curtain tie backs. When this treatment is deemed too "girly," it's easy to remove it and streamline the bedroom.

WOW WITH TILES

(Below left) Playing with tile, stone, and mosaic elements to create a wow factor bathroom is akin to solving a puzzle. In one of the kid's bathrooms, a field of cloud-blue glazed tiles surrounds an inset panel of powder blue and white marble mosaic in a graphic chevron pattern.

PRETTY PALETTE

(Above right) With views to the east over the forest and field, this room is bright and breezy. Barely there wispy green and blue hues feel springy and fresh. The bed and bedside tables were vintage store finds, and the framed bookplates above the bed were found for five dollars each at a flea market.

CURTAIN CALL

(Below right) Looking to add privacy to the bathroom yet let the light wash in? Patterned eyelet dressmaking fabric was sewn into a pair of flat panel drapes to lend texture and softness to the bathtub area.

"No matter how big or small your house, there will always be concessions. A second-floor laundry was a priority, and so was a home office/crafting space for me and the girls. With big windows and lots of natural light, this room is the ultimate double-duty space. If I'm working, I don't run the laundry, so it's a great compromise, not to mention a fluff and fold zone with a pretty sweet view."
—SR

↓
The cabinetry in the laundry room features shutter panel door fronts in pale aqua, vintage brass hardware, and open shelves for folded items supported on reproduction brass brackets. When it's time to sort a fresh load of laundry, grab baskets for each family member to make it easy.

→
The laundry/office is separated from the hall by a reclaimed carriage house door that slides on a barn door track. If you want to use architectural salvage as a feature, be sure to shop for it in the earliest stage of your project so you can build to accomodate the size of what you find. This is one of a pair—the door was made extra wide to accomodate it, and the mate was installed in the media room.

↓
In the home of a designer, media room doesn't necessarily mean "man cave"—harnessing a palette of natural linen and flax mixed with indigo and denim blue makes the hangout space fuss free yet bright and fresh.

"THIS IS OUR FOURTH TOTAL REDO OF A HOUSE; I'VE LOVED THEM ALL, BUT NONE AS MUCH AS THIS WOOD-FRAME QUEEN ANNE. IT'S SPECIAL FROM THE FRONT PORCH RIGHT UP TO THE ROOFLINE."

Storybook Victorian

DESIGN BY **SCOTT FRANCISCO**,
JANE FRANCISCO, AND **COLIN FAULKNER**
PHOTOGRAPHY BY **COLIN FAULKNER**

DESIGN
BY **SCOTT
FRANCISCO**,
PILOT PROJECTS
DESIGN,
**JANE
FRANCISCO
& COLIN
FAULKNER**

GLEN RIDGE,
NEW JERSEY

5,000 SQUARE
FEET

135 YEARS OLD

2-YEAR
RENOVATION

7 BEDROOMS

5 BATHROOMS

10-FOOT
CEILINGS

3 KITCHEN
SINKS

↓
The front hall's a master class in making an entrance. Faceted built-ins were designed to look original and match the striking front door. (Fun fact: The exterior mail slot goes through to a niche inside!) Crisp white paint, quarter-sawn white oak floors installed in a herringbone pattern, and mid-century-style furniture and lighting signal this old house is full of new tricks.

IT ALL STARTED with a porch. When Jane Francisco, editor in chief of *Good Housekeeping*, and her husband, photographer Colin Faulkner, were looking for a place to put down roots within a forty-five-minute commute to her work in Manhattan, they were drawn to this leafy town in New Jersey, where some streets are still lit with gas lamps. "A lot of the houses here were built twenty to thirty years before the turn of the century and many had gorgeous porches," Jane says. "A porch wasn't the only priority but it was definitely in the mix—we've never had one." Jane and Colin were no strangers to down-to-the-studs renovations, having done three before. Still, they were pleased to find the circa 1885 Victorian was in great shape—until contractors pointed out the plumbing, electrical, and HVAC needed to be replaced. Oh, and then there was the furnace and roof. What began as a minor makeover turned into a major overhaul: out went every wire, pipe, and tube and many of the walls along with them. In spite of the surprises, the two-year journey has a happy ending complete with an airy, open floor plan, new windows, and a to-die-for cook's kitchen, to name a few highlights. "From the high ceilings and abundant light, to the room for family and friends to stay, and yes, the front porch, this house combines all the best attributes of our previous homes into one," says Colin.

"When we started the renovation, we weren't going to spend the money to replace the floors, but it's one of the changes that really makes this level of the house. A barely there white stain removed the pink and yellow from the oak to give us the light, airy, and bright feeling we were after."

—Jane Francisco

↓
Curved walls both inside and outside the house—a hallmark of Queen Anne Victorian-style architecture—are part of what make it so unique and dreamy. A visual threshold can be easily created with strips of flooring to break up the pattern and separate one zone from another.

YES, YOU CAN!

Add modern lines to an older home by removing the crown moulding but keeping the original window casings and baseboards.

A pared-back palette of white, black, and natural looks perennially fresh when placed inside a traditional envelope. And if it ain't broke, don't change it! "We've always stuck with white, grey, and black," says Jane. "It's just what both of us really like and we don't get tired of it."

Learning from previous kitchen renos informed Jane and Colin's choices on this one. Their foolproof formula? Four counter surfaces—marble, black walnut, stainless, and granite—that look cohesive, a hardworking sink, simple lines, and a limited palette.

DETAILS WE LOVE

1- The black walnut cutting board inset on the honed Calacatta marble island adds warmth and functionality: "Yes, we really use that cutting board every day," says Jane.

2- An industrial-style interior window has three smart functions: It hides a support beam, provides a backdrop for the hood, and separates the space without closing it off.

3- Looking to keep clutter off the counters? Run a durable stainless ledge around the perimeter to hold spices and gadgets.

4- When the kitchen's in the middle of the house—and visible from every main-floor room—a triple sink maintains the appearance of tidiness without having every dish washed.

5- Patterned encaustic floor tiles and hand-glazed wall tiles add a soulful, artisanal touch.

Cabinet Colour: Black Panther (2125-10) by Benjamin Moore

YES, YOU CAN!

Make an all-white room feel warm and cozy with natural-fibre rugs, rich wood, and an infusion of gold tones.

↑
When your house is set back from the road, why bother with window treatments? Let the light pour in and bounce off white walls and furniture for the brightest, sunniest space possible. "We're slowly trying to figure out what's necessary," says Colin. "But the reality is, they'd be open 99 percent of the time anyway."

→
A stainless steel–topped bar area acts as a transition between the kitchen and entertaining zone. A sink, fridge, and dishwasher drawers keep all the glassware and cocktail fixings self-contained.

An iconic Eero Saarinen table, one of Jane and Colin's prize vintage possessions, looks serene against one of Colin's own framed photographs, shot on the Georgian Bay side of Ontario's Bruce Peninsula. Jane found the ceiling pendant online and liked its organic shape. "Mod light fixtures in rooms with traditional bones is definitely one of our go-to things," she says.

Wall + Trim Colour:
Paper White (OC-55) by Benjamin Moore

← When you've got five bathrooms to renovate, creativity counts and budget solutions are a bonus. Jane and Colin turned a retro teak credenza with sleek built-in handles into a lean vanity for the powder room and installed inky grasscloth wallpaper as a moody backdrop.

→ Play with opposites in a guest room for a welcoming look that's anything but cookie-cutter. A mid-century chair is right at home beside a sweet, flea-market side table—shades of white unify pieces of different design eras.

"When I'm not travelling, this is my office and I spend most of my days up here. The space is filled with light all day long and if I want, I can open the porch door and step outside, or let the breezes blow through." —Colin Faulkner

YES, YOU CAN!
Make a nothing-special subfloor look like a million bucks with high-gloss enamel paint.

↓
Sometimes, the best idea is to side with history. These windows are the only ones in the house that weren't replaced—their single-paned wavy glass and elaborate mullions are perfect in their imperfection.

↓
The whitewashed third floor loft with exposed rafters is Colin's creative workroom. Like an inspiration board come to life, the airy space is filled with vintage furniture and found objects (he loves to pin branches and pictures to the wall), and evokes the vibe of an industrial warehouse feeling in a nineteenth-century house.

Floor Colour:
White Wisp (OC-54) by Benjamin Moore

Collected Source Guide

DESIGNER DIRECTORY
(In order of appearance)

Sarah Richardson Design
sarahrichardson design.com

Suzanne Dimma Design
suzannedimma.com

Arriz + Co
arrizandco.com

Tharon Anderson
tharonanderson design.com

Anna Spiro Design
annaspiro design.com.au

Dee Murphy
murphydeesign.com

Jenny Keenan Design
jennykeenan design.com

Ashton Klomp Interiors
ashtonklomp.com

Sophie Burke Design
sophieburke design.com

Heather Chadduck Interiors
heatherchadduck .com

Three Birds Renovations
threebirds renovations.com

Chango & Co.
chango.co

Scott Francisco
pilot-projects.org

"APRÈS-SKI? MAIS OUI!" pages 4 to 21
GENERAL First Class Flooring: engineered floors, firstclassflooring.ca | Normerica: timber home design, normerica.com.

LIVING ROOM Sarah Richardson for Palliser: Promenade sectional, Promenade chaise, Stride swivel chair, Silhouette chair, Annex duplex dining table, Annex hex storage cocktail table, Shore veranda end table, Courtyard square and round leather ottomans, Crosswalk rug, Hopscotch pillow, Stitch pillow, Laneway throw, Strie throw, sarahrichardson.palliser.com | Invisirail: glass railing system, invisirail.com | IKEA: NYMÅNE swing arm wall lamp, SANELA light blue cushion cover, VÄRMER tray, FENOMEN candles, ikea.com | Kravet: accent pillow fabrics, Lee Jofa Aslin Teal, Lee Jofa Arlo Indigo, kravet.com | HomeSense: table lamp, vases, homesense.ca | Dulux: beam paint Universal Grey 00NN 62/000, dulux.com | Benjamin Moore: wall paint, Seapearl OC-19, benjaminmoore.com.

KITCHEN IKEA: GRIMSLÖV series kitchen cabinetry, VÄXJÖ pendant lamps, ÄLMAREN stainless steel coloured kitchen faucet, KASKER quartz white stone countertop, sink, ARBETE decorative bowl, ikea.com | Saltillo: Herringbone Carrara Marble Mosaic backsplash, floor tiles, saltillo-tiles.com | Structube: LARS Elmwood Iron Stool, structube.com | Benjamin Moore: wall paint Chantilly Lace OC-65, benjaminmoore.com | Home Depot: Richelieu knobs, homedepot.ca | Tasco Appliances: KitchenAid stove, KitchenAid fridge, KitchenAid dishwasher, tascoappliance .ca | Dags & Willow: Ottercreek Woodworks large wooden cheese board (on counter), dagsandwillow.ca | Indigo: large round cutting board, chapters.indigo.ca | HomeSense: small cutting board with round handle, homesense.ca | Real Canadian Superstore: white bowls, realcanadiansuperstore.ca | Jong Young Flower Market: large vase, jongyoungflowermarket.ca.

DINING ROOM Sarah Richardson for Palliser: Annex rectangular dining table, Annex credenza, Shore boardwalk side chair, Shore mirror, Boulevard arch armchair, Pinwheel rug, sarahrichardson.palliser.com | Invisirail: glass railing system, invisirail.com | Shop Sarah Richardson: Birch marble napkins, sarahrichardsondesign.com | IKEA: dinnerware sets, placemats, ikea.com | Real Canadian Superstore: glassware, realcanadiansuperstore.ca | Wayfair: pendant, wayfair.ca | HomeSense: Ralph Lauren lamps, homesense.ca | Benjamin Moore: wall paint, Seapearl OC-19, benjaminmoore.com | Dulux: beam paint Universal Grey 00NN 62/000, dulux.com.

GUEST BATH The Rubinet Faucet Company: GENESIS series faucets, rubinet.com | Saltillo: marble mosaic tiles, saltillo-tiles.com | Renwil: vanity mirror, renwil.com | CB2: Desmond antique mirror sconces, cb2.ca | IKEA: towels, ikea.com | American Standard: toilet, americanstandard.ca | West Elm: vases, westelm .com | Home Depot: Jade bath, homedepot.ca | Dinuovo Granite & Marble Inc.: remnant marble countertop, tub backsplash, window shelf, dinuovo.ca | Kohler: sink, kohler.ca | HomeSense: round mirror, homesense.ca | Benjamin Moore: wall and ceiling paint, Wickham Gray HC-171, benjaminmoore.com.

PRINCIPAL BEDROOM Sarah Richardson for Palliser: Shore Collection arch chair, Vista Collection round end table, Courtyard Collection ellipse ottoman, Facet rug in cream, sarahrichardson.palliser.com | IKEA: BJÖRKSNÄS bed frame, PAX storage system, BERGPALM duvet cover and pillowcase(s), ikea.com | Lowe's: Richelieu closet hardware, lowes.ca | Minted: art print, minted .com | Wayfair: pendant, wayfair.ca | HomeSense: lamps, baskets with lid, homesense .ca | Kravet: accent pillow fabrics, kravet.com | Elte Mkt: white marble bowls, eltemkt.com | Benjamin Moore: wall paint, Balboa Mist, OC-27, benjaminmoore.com.

PRINCIPAL ENSUITE IKEA: GODMORGON vanity, OTTAVA brass pendant lamp, ROTSUND mirror, picture frames, countertop, towels, ikea .com | Kohler: sink, kohler.ca | The Rubinet Faucet Company: Raven series shower system and faucet, rubinet.com | Saltillo: all tiles, saltillo-tiles.com | John Audubon: Birds of America, Plate 295 Manks Sherwater + Plate 299 Dusky Petrel, audubon.org | True North Glass Co.: glass shower enclosure, tngc.ca | Wayfair: brass vanity hardware, wayfair.ca | Benjamin Moore: wall and ceiling paint, Chantilly Lace, OC-65, benjaminmoore.com.

GIRL'S ROOM Sarah Richardson for Palliser: Horizon chair, throw blanket, Zig Zag teal rug, Shore bedroom collection, sarahrichardson .palliser.com | Minted: art prints, wall mural, accent pillows, minted.com | Wayfair: lamps, wayfair.ca | Sarah Richardson for Kravet: lumbar pillow fabric "Highpoint Pool," sarahrichardsondesign.com | Premier Prints: Roman blind fabric "Pebbles Caribbean, Scott Living," premierprints.com | IKEA: duvet cover set "Ofelia Vass," frames, hooks, work lamp "FORSÅ lamp," ikea.com | West Elm: small and large vases, westelm.com | Benjamin Moore: beams and ceiling paint, Chantilly Lace OC-65, benjaminmoore.com.

LOWER LEVEL BATH Sarah Richardson for Brewster: Ziggity Aegean Grasscloth wallpaper, **sarahrichardsondesign.com** | Saltillo: shower and floor tiles, **saltillo-tiles.com** | True North Glass Co.: glass shower enclosure, **tngc.ca** | Minted: Sea Glass art print, **minted.com** | The Rubinet Faucet Company: Hexis series faucet, shower system, towel bar, **rubinet.com** | Kohler: Verticyl rectangle undermount bathroom sink, **kohler.ca** | IKEA: vanity, light pendant, towel bar, hooks, towels, picture frame, **ikea.com** | Renwil: Tia metal mirror, **renwil.com** | Richelieu: vanity hardware, **richelieu.com** | Benjamin Moore: beams and ceiling paint, Chantilly Lace OC-65, **benjaminmoore.com**.

LOWER HALL Sarah Richardson for Palliser: Courtyard quilted round ottomans, **sarahrichardson.palliser.com** | Invisirail: glass railing system, **invisirail.com** | Minted: art prints, "Ice on the Lake," "Ice Age," "Brush in Turquoise," **minted.com** | Brewster Home Fashions: Runes Seafoam Brushstrokes wallpaper 2764-24356, **brewsterwallcovering.com** | IKEA: picture frames, **ikea.com** | Lowe's: cabinetry hardware, **lowes.ca** | Gray Malin: Park City Skiers photograph, **graymalin.com** | Glidden: closet door paint, Quiet Rain 50BG 64/028, **glidden.com** | Dulux: beam and stair paint, Universal Grey 00NN 62/000, **dulux.com** | Benjamin Moore: beams and ceiling paint, Chantilly Lace OC-65, **benjaminmoore.com**.

MEDIA ROOM Sarah Richardson for Palliser: Silhouette sofa, Vista rectangular cocktail table, Annex round end tables, Boulevard tall salon table, Trilogy rug, Hopscotch charcoal pillows, Hopscotch and Laneway throw blankets, **sarahrichardson.palliser.com** | Sarah Richardson for Brewster: Ziggity Linen wallpaper 2785-24817, **sarahrichardsondesign.com** | Enviro: EX35 gas fireplace insert, **enviro.com** | Crate & Barrel: grass circular art on fireplace, **crateandbarrel.ca** | Minted: Matchstick Black and Pattern Play accent pillows, **minted.com** | IKEA: HEKTAR floor lamps, **ikea.com** | Kiondo African Imports Inc.: bowl with lid, **kiondo.com** | Wayfair: pendant, **wayfair.ca** | Glidden: ceiling paint, Early Evening PPG1006-3, **glidden.com**.

MUDROOM Minted: accent pillows, **minted.com** | IKEA: PUDDA baskets, FLÅDIS seagrass baskets, **ikea.com** | Abbott: Large industrial hook, 27-IRON AGE/276, **abbottcollection.com** | HomeSense: striped baskets, **homesense.ca** | Universal: tracking lighting, **greatlighting.com** | Sherwin-Williams: ceiling and beams paint, Argos SW 7065, **sherwin-williams.com**.

"REMAKING HISTORY," pages 22 to 37
LIVING ROOM Forbes & Lomax: brass switchplates, **forbesandlomax.com** | Y&Co: area rug, white throw pillow, **ycocarpet.com** | Hopson Grace: Rina Menardi vase, **hopsongrace.com**.

ENTRY Hollace Cluny: black stool, **hollacecluny.ca**.

DINING ROOM NewWall: Timorous Beasties Indie Wood wallpaper, **newwall.com**.

POWDER ROOM Y&Co: Galbraith & Paul wallpaper, **ycocarpet.com**.

HALLWAY Kiondo African Imports: beaded crown, **kiondo.com** | Klaus by Nienkamper, brass dish, **klausn.com**.

DEN Hollacy Cluny: tan leather chair, small caned chair, table lamp, throw, **hollacecluny.ca** | Klaus by Nienkamper, brass dish, wood table, **klausn.com** | Avenue Road: side table, **avenue-road.com** | Y&Co: blue pillow, **ycocarpet.com** | Hopson Grace: floor cushion, **hopsongrace.com**.

BEDROOM Y&Co: striped pillow, **ycocarpet.com** | Au Lit Fine Linens: all other bedding by Suzanne Dimma capsule collection, **aulitfinelinens.com**.

BATHROOM Article 27: pink hand towel, pink bath towel, sponge, **art27.ca** | Coriander Girl: flowers on vanity, **coriandergirl.com**.

"FIRESIDE RUSTIC," pages 38 to 47
GREAT ROOM Sarah Richardson Design: Cory sofa, Matthew dining chairs, Thomas stool, Ruth chaise, **sarahrichardsondesign.com** | Bilbrough: Sofa fabric, curtain fabric, **bilbroughs.com** | Lee Jofa: Dining chair fabric, pillow fabrics, **kravet.com** | Primavera Interior Furnishings: chaise fabric, **primaverafurnishings.com** | Y & Co.: stool fabric, rug, **ycocarpet.com** | Elte: side tables, table lamps, floor lamps, chandelier, **elte.com** | Restoration Hardware: coffee table, **restorationhardware.com** | Hopson Grace: candle sticks, **hopsongrace.com** | Cabinet Furniture: games table, **cabinetfurniture.ca** | The Door Store: vintage horses, **thedoorstore.ca** | Peaks and Rafters: side table, decorative bowl, **peaksandrafters.com** | Renaissance Fireplaces: Rumford wood burning fireplace, **renaissancefireplaces.com** | Benjamin Moore: wall stain colour, Collingwood OC-28, **benjaminmoore.com**.

PRINCIPAL BEDROOM Sarah Richardson Design: Taylor king bed, Kieran bench, Lola chairs, Selena stool, **sarahrichardsondesign.com** | Kravet: headboard fabric, curtains, **kravet.com** | Kobe Interior Products: mohair pillow, **kobefabrics.com** | Bilbrough: lumbar pillow, chair fabric, **bilbroughs.com** | Serena & Lily: bedding,

www.serenaandlily.com | Elte: table lamps, floor lamp, rug, elte.com | Boo Boo and Lefty: Nightstands, boobooandlefty.com | Robert Allen: bench fabric, stool fabric, robertallendesign.com | Canvas Gallery: Meredith Bingham artwork, canvasgallery.ca | Y & Co.: pillow fabric, ycocarpet.com | Universal Lighting: side table, greatlighting.com | CB2: white pouf, cb2.ca | Kathy Richardson: artwork, kathyrichardsonphotography.ca | Pottery Barn: quilt, potterybarn.ca | Woven Treasures: hide rug, facebook.com/WovenTreasuresToronto | Benjamin Moore: wall stain colour, Collingwood OC-28, benjaminmoore.com.

GUEST BATHROOM Northern Living Kitchen and Bath: vanity, northernlivingkitchenandbath.ca | Taps: plumbing fixtures, tapsbath.com | Upper Canada Specialty Hardware: cabinet hardware, ucshshowroom.com | Wayfair: sconces, wayfair.ca | Elgin Picture and Frame: custom mirrors, elginpictureandframe.com | Saltillo Imports: tile, www.saltillo-tiles.com | Kravet: roman blind fabric, kravet.com | Elte Market: canisters, elte.com | Home Sense: towels, homesense.ca.

GUEST BEDROOM Sarah Richardson Design: Nicola queen bed, sarahrichardsondesign.com | Lee Jofa: bed fabric, kravet.com | Kravet: accent pillows, kravet.com | Bungalow 5: nightstands, bungalow5.com | Wayfair: sconces, wayfair.ca | Canvas Gallery, Ian Varney: artwork .canvasgallery.ca | Serena & Lily: bedding, serenaandlily.com.

HALLWAY Dash & Albert: rugs, annieselke.com | West Elm: picture frames, westelm.com | Union Lighting: star flush mount, unionlightingandfurnishings.com | Lee Jofa: pillow fabric, kravet.com | Emtek: door hardware, emtek.com | Kathy Richardson: artwork, kathyrichardsonphotography.ca | Serena & Lily: bedding, serenaandlily.com.

"BEHIND THE DUNES," pages 48 to 63
ENTRYWAY Studio Four: Sally King-Benedict wallpaper, studiofournyc.com | Circa Lighting: Kelly Wearstler lamp, circalighting.com.

DINING ROOM Catherine Booker Jones: artwork, catherinejonesstudio.com.

PRINCIPAL BEDROOM Stark Carpet: custom jute rug, starkcarpet.com.

GIRL'S ROOM Lulie Wallace: wallpaper, luliewallace.com.

POOL HOUSE BEDROOM Room & Board: bed, roomandboard.com.

"OLD SOUL, NEW START," pages 86 to 101
LIVING ROOM Stark Carpet: custom rug, starkcarpet.com | West Elm: throw pillows, westelm.com | Uprise Art: artwork, upriseart.com | CB2: sectional, cb2.com | Aguirre Design: console tables, mauricioaguirre.com | First Dibs: TR Bulb lamps, 1stdibs.com.

PRINCIPAL BEDROOM Restoration Hardware: bed, restorationhardware.com | Groundwork Home: nightstands, groundworkhome.com | CFC: console table, customefurniturela.com | Uprise Art: artwork, upriseart.com | Arteriors: bench, arteriorshome.com | CB2: chair, mirror, cb2.com | West Elm: desk, westelm.com | The Future Perfect: lamp, thefutureperfect.com.

NURSERY Studio Four NYC: wallpaper, studiofournyc.com | Pottery Barn Teen: daybed, pbteen.com | Anthropologie: rocking chair, anthropologie.com | Maisonette: animal heads, maisonette.com.

BOY'S ROOM Decorator's Best: wallpaper, decoratorsbest.com | CB2: bed, cb2.com | Crate & Barrel: nightstands, crateandbarrel.com | Y Living: table lamps, yliving.com | Mecox: accent chair, mecox.com.

"WRITTEN IN THE STARS," pages 102 to 119
GENERAL Robinson Residential: architectural design, robinsonplans.com | Metrie: interior doors, panelling, trim, metrie.com | Strassburger: windows and doors, strassburger.net | Emtek: door hardware and hinges, emtek.com | Rehau: in-floor heating system, rehau.com | Barwood: flooring, barwoodfloors.com.

LIVING ROOM Sarah Richardson for Palliser: Highland Rug, sarahrichardson.palliser.com | Wayfair: side table, table lamp, star sculpture, armchair, ottoman, side chair, mirror, club chair, sofa, wayfair.ca | The Door Store: capital fragment, thedoorstore.ca | Renaissance Fireplaces: fireplace, renaissancefireplaces.com | Crystal Tile: fireplace surround, crystaltilemarble.com | Sarah Richardson Design custom furniture: Kitty chairs, Victoria chairs, sarahrichardsondesign.com | Sarah Richardson Design for Kravet: Kitty chair fabric (Granby Stone), Victoria chair fabric (Zig and Zag Silver), drapery fabric (Latticely, Pewter), sarahrichardsondesign.com | Thibaut: wallpaper, thibautdesign.com | Circa Lighting: chandelier, circalighting.com | Vintage Fine Objects: painting, sconces, accessories, vintagefineobjects.com | Absolutely Inc.: swirl side table, absolutelyinc.com | Elte: coffee table, elte.com | Kiondo: spider stool, teardrop stool, kiondo.com | Glidden: wall paint, Meeting House White 50YY 74/069, glidden.com.

EXTERIOR Maibec: wood siding on house, maibec.com | Vicwest: roof, vicwest.com | Beaver Valley Stone: masonal stone, stone veneer supply, beavervalleystone.ca | Mason's Masonry Supply Ltd.: pool surround, masonsmasonry.com | Thornbury Clear Choice Pools & Spas: pool, thornburyclearchoice.com | Fox Pools: clear deck, foxpool.com | Hauser: outdoor furniture, hauserstores.com | Wayfair: outdoor planters, wayfair.ca | Joel Loblaw: landscape design, joelloblaw.com | Post Farm Structures: exterior, postfarm.ca | Sentinel Solar: solar products, sentinelsolar.com.

STAIR LANDING Saltillo Tiles: natural stone flooring, saltillo-tiles.com | Sarah Richardson for Kravet: drapery fabric (Sarouk Rug, pumice), sarahrichardsondesign.com | Kravet: accent pillow fabric, kravet.com | Stairhaus: supply and install of stairs and railings, stairhaus.com | A&D Wood Turning: railings, restoration of newel posts, adwoodturning.com | Artefacts: antique newel posts, artefacts.ca | The Door Store: columns, thedoorstore.ca | Elle & Eve: pair of chairs, elleandeve.ca | Tonic Living: chair fabric, tonicliving.ca | Around the Block: accessories, aroundtheblock.com | Dulux: wall paint, Tulle White 50BG 72/006, dulux.ca.

DEN/OFFICE Sarah Richardson for Palliser: Vantage sofa, Vista square end table, Ellipse large round ottoman, sarahrichardson.palliser.com | Renaissance Fireplaces: Rumford 1000 fireplace insert, renaissancefireplaces.com | Saltillo Tile Imports: mosaic fireplace surround, saltillo-tiles.com | Wayfair: table lamp, rug, wayfair.ca | Artefacts: antique trim panel used as mantel, artefacts.ca | Sarah Richardson Design for Kravet: drapery fabric (Decowaves, pumice), sarahrichardsondesign.com | Kravet: accent pillow (Leyla-1611, dove), kravet.com | Tonic Living: accent pillow, tonicliving.ca | Vintage Fine Objects: tub chair, vintagefineobjects.com | Universal Lighting: sconces, greatlighting.com | Of Things Past: mirror, ofthingspast.com | Crate & Barrel: game, crateandbarrel.com | Dulux: wall paint, Snowfield 00NN 72/000, dulux.ca.

KITCHEN Wayfair: wall sconce, bar stool, pendant, wayfair.ca | Monogram: appliances, monogram.ca | Cabico: Elmwood series cabinetry, cabico.com | Saltillo Tile: backsplash, floor, fireplace surround, saltillo-tiles.com | Caesarstone: countertops, caesarstone.ca | Waterstone: kitchen faucets, waterstoneco.com | Blanco: kitchen sinks, blanco.com | Sarah Richardson Design: Margo side chairs, sarahrichardsondesign.com | Sarah Richardson Design for Kravet: fabric for vintage chairs (Granby, stone), accent pillow fabric (Wavelink, pewter), accent pillow fabric (Harbord, linen), accent pillow fabric (Diamond Dots, linen), sarahrichardsondesign.com | Kravet: accent pillow fabric, kravet.com | Smash Salvage: white bowls, ceramic flush mount lights, smashsalvage.com | Vintage Fine Objects: small wooden stool, vintagefineobjects.com | Lee Valley: octagonal knobs, leevalley.com | Upper Canada Hardware: modern hex pull, ucshshowroom.com | Glidden: wall paint, Natural White 50YY 83/029, glidden.com | CIL: ceiling paint, White On White 30GY 88/014, cil.ca | Benjamin Moore: millwork paint, Stonington Gray HC-170, benjaminmoore.com.

DINING ROOM Wayfair: armchairs, flatware set, wayfair.ca | Sarah Richardson for Kravet: drapery fabric (Peony Tree, aquamarine), accent pillow fabric (Lineweave, breeze, and Wavelink, glacier), napkin fabric (Sarouk Rug, Aquamarine), sarahrichardsondesign.com | Around the Block: brass candlesticks, various white ceramics, aroundtheblock.com | Vintage Fine Objects: various white ceramics, vintagefineobjects.com | Of Things Past: various white ceramics, ofthingspast.com | Artefacts: dining table, artefacts.ca | Smash Salvage: antique store counter buffet, smashsalvage.com | Crystal Tile & Marble: marble on counter buffer, crystaltilemarble.com | Elte: chandelier, elte.com | Elmwood Kitchens: millwork, cabico.com | Lee Valley: octagonal knobs, leevalley.com | CIL: wall paint, Natural White 50YY 83/029, cil.ca | Glidden: ceiling paint, White On White 30GY 88/014, glidden.com.

SUNROOM Wayfair: ottoman, end table, rug, wayfair.ca | Sarah Richardson Design: Cory sofa, Lola chairs, Thomas stools, throw blanket, sarahrichardsondesign.com | Sarah Richardson Design for Kravet: sofa fabric (Lineweave, dune), chair fabric (Ikat Strie, pewter), accent pillow fabric (Mod Peaks, silver), sarahrichardsondesign.com | Kravet: drapery fabric (Branches, sand), accent pillow fabric (Gerbera, silver), kravet.com | Tonic Living: accent pillow fabric, tonicliving.com | Of Things Past: glass lantern, brass bowl, ofthingspast.com | Saltillo Tiles: natural stone flooring, saltillo-tiles.com | Rehau: in-floor heating system, rehau.com | Kiondo: stool, kiondo.com | Vintage Fine Objects: table lamps, vintagefineobjects.com | Glidden: wall paint, White on White 30GY 88/014, glidden.com | CIL: ceiling paint, Toasted White 40YY 73/028, cil.ca.

LAUNDRY ROOM Elmwood Kitchens: millwork, elmwoodkitchens.com | Caesarstone: counter top, pure white, caesarstone.ca | Dinuovo Granite & Marble Inc: counter fabrication and install, **yellowpages.ca** | GE: washer & dryer, **geappliances.ca** | Taps/Rubinet: brass faucet, **tapsbath.com** | Taps/Blanco: stainless steel sink, **blanco.com** | The Door Store: vintage carriage house door, cabinet hardware, brass brackets, **thedoorstore.ca** | Vintage Fine Objects: faux bois chair, **vintagefineobjects.com** | Sarah Richardson for Kravet: fabric for chair (Granby, chambray), accent pillow (Geo Floral, grotto), **sarahrichardsondesign.com** | Wayfair: mini-pendant, towels, **wayfair.ca** | Ikea: rug, **ikea.com** | West Elm: blue vase, **westelm.com** | Canadian Tire: baskets, **canadiantire.ca** | Benjamin Moore: wall paint, White Wisp 2137-70, cabinetry paint, Harbor Haze 2136-60, **benjaminmoore.com** | Glidden: trim and baseboards, White On White 30GY 88/014, **glidden.com**.

GREEN BEDROOM: Sarah Richardson Design: throw, bedding, **sarahrichardsondesign.com** | Sarah Richardson for Kravet: drapery fabric (Latticely, jade), chair fabric (Decowaves, jade), **sarahrichardsondesign.com** | Wayfair: table lamp, quilt set, **wayfair.com** | Elle & Eve: bed frame, chandelier, **elleandeve.ca** | Thibaut: accent pillow on bed, **thibautdesign.com** | Dulux: wall paint, Forest Light 30GY 83/064, **dulux.ca**.

BLUE BEDROOM: Thibaut: accent pillows, accent pillow fabric, **thibautdesign.com** | Sarah Richardson Design: bedding, accent pillows, throw blanket, **sarahrichardsondesign.com** | Wayfair: nightstand, headboard, chandelier, quilt set, **wayfair.ca** | The Door Store: hardware on side tables, canopy tie backs, **thedoorstore.ca**.

PRINCIPAL BATHROOM Saltillo Tile Imports: all marble tile, flooring, mosaic, **saltillo-tiles.com** | Elmwood Kitchens: custom vanity with makeup table, **elmwoodkitchens.com** | Taps/Hansgrohe: axor montreux faucets/shower systems/towel bars, **tapsbath.com** | Taps/Alcove: cosmos freestanding tub, **tapsbath.com** | Taps/Kohler: verticyl K-2881 sink, **tapsbath.com** | Crystal Tile: countertop and jambs, **crystaltilemarble.com** | Decorum: mirrors, **ddfhome.net** | Residential Lighting: vintage italian sconce, **residentiallightingstudio.com** | Sarah Richardson for Kravet: drapery fabric (Dropsheer, cream), **sarahrichardsondesign.com** | Elte Mkt: foot stool, **eltemkt.com** | The Door Store: glass pendants, vanity hardware and hooks, **thedoorstore.ca** | Dulux: wall paint, White wisteria 70BB 73/020, **dulux.ca**.

PRINCIPAL BEDROOM Sarah Richardson Design: headboard, chairs, stool, **sarahrichardsondesign.com** | Sarah Richardson for Kravet: stool fabric (Kittycat, aquamarine), chairs (All Star, ivory), drapery and accent pillow fabric (Ginkgo Leaf, mist), **sarahrichardsondesign.com** | Wayfair: nightstand, chest, table lamp, quilt set, rug, mirror, **wayfair.ca** | Post & Beam Architectural Reclamation: carved wood ceiling panel, **pandb .ca** | Residential Lighting: silver chandelier, **residentiallightingstudio.com** | Dulux: wall paint, Chelsea Fog 10GG 72/022, panel inlay paint, Natural White 50YY 83/029, **dulux.ca**.

MEDIA ROOM Brunswick: pool table, **brunswickbilliards.com** | Pacific Energy Woodstoves: wood stove, **pacificenergy.net** | Fiber and Cloth: engineered wood floors, **fiberandcloth.com** | Monogram: bar fridges, **monogram.ca** | Caesarstone: counter top, clamshell, **caesarstone.ca** | Dinuovo Granite & Marble Inc: counter fabrication and install, **dinuovo.ca** | Saltillo: star tile, **saltillo-tiles .com** | Elgin Picture and Frame: framing, **elginpictureandframe.com** | Toronto Image Works: fine art printing, **torontoimageworks .com** | Taps: stainless steel sink and faucet, matte black, **tapsbath.com** | Sarah Richardson Design: Emma chairs, **sarahrichardsondesign .com** | Sarah Richardson for Kravet: chair fabric (Zig and Zag, indigo), drapery accent and pillow fabric (Granby, lake), **sarahrichardsondesign .com** | Kravet: pillow fabric, **kravet.com** | Wayfair: table lamp, club chair, coffee table, bar stools, throw pillows, sofa, bench, end table, rug, pendants, mirror, **wayfair.com** | Elte: monaco round tufted ottoman, grey, **elte .com** | Crystal Tile Marble: coffee table top, **crystaltilemarble.com** | Artefacts: coffee table base, **artefacts.ca** | Lowe's: cabinets, **lowes.ca** | Kiondo: indigo throw, **kiondo.com** | Around the Block: vases, **aroundtheblock.com** | Universal Lighting: desk lamp, **greatlighting.com** | Dulux: wall and ceiling paint, Natural White 0YY 83/029, **dulux.ca**.

"STORYBOOK VICTORIAN," pages 120 to 133
ENTRYWAY West Elm: table, **westelm .com** | Lucent Lightshop: ceiling fixture, **lucentlightshop.com** | Hay: sofa, **hay.dk/en-ca** | Benjamin Moore: wall paint, Paper White OC-55, **benjaminmoore.com**.

FAMILY ROOM Lawa: ceiling pendant, **lawadesign .dk** | Benjamin Moore: wall paint, Paper White OC-55, **benjaminmoore.com**.

KITCHEN Moroccan Mosaic & Tile House: floor tiles, **mosaicmorocco.com** | Tile Bar: wall tiles, **tilebar.com** | Design Within Reach: ceiling pendants, **dwr.com** | New Jersey Stone: marble counter, granite stove, **newjerseystone.com** | BCB Stainless: custom sinks with drainboards, **bcbstainlesssteelnyc.com** | Miele: induction stovetop, **miele.com**.

LIVING ROOM ABC Home: chair, **abchome.com** | IKEA: rug, **ikea.com** | Alex Raskin Antiques: mirror, **alexraskinantiques.com** | Benjamin Moore: wall paint, Paper White OC-55, **benjaminmoore.com**.

DINING ROOM Vitra: chairs, **vitra.com** | 2Modern: ceiling fixture, **2modern.com** | Colin Faulkner: photograph, **faulknerphoto.com**.

LOFT STUDIO West Elm: ceiling fixture, **westelm .com** | IKEA: love seat, **ikea.com** | Flos: table lamp, **flos.com** | Benjamin Moore: wall paint, Paper White OC-55, floor paint, White Wisp OC-54, **benjaminmoore.com**.